# The Point of Inconvenience

A.F. Harrold was born in Sussex in 1975 and has lived in Reading since the mid-nineties. He writes a wide variety of verse and prose, for both adults and children.

# The Point
# of Inconvenience

*A. F. Harrold*

TWO
RIVERS
PRESS

First published in the UK in 2013 by Two Rivers Press
7 Denmark Road, Reading RG1 5PA.
www.tworiverspress.com

ISBN 978-1-901677-90-4

1 2 3 4 5 6 7 8 9

Two Rivers Press is represented in the UK by Inpress Ltd
and distributed by Central Books.

Cover design by Sally Castle.
Text design by Nadja Guggi and typeset in Janson and Parisine.

Printed and bound in Great Britain by Imprint Digital, Exeter.

*for my brother*

*in memory of our mother*
*Ann Frances Harrold*
*28/10/1945 – 07/05/2010*

*By the same author:*

Poetry
*Logic And The Heart* (Two Rivers Press, 2004)
*Of Birds And Bees* (Quirkstandard's Alternative, 2008)
*Flood* (Two Rivers Press, 2010)

Entertainments
*Postcards From The Hedgehog* (Two Rivers Press, 2007)
*The Man Who Spent Years In The Bath* (Quirkstandard's
    Alternative, 2008)
*The Education Of Epitome Quirkstandard* (Quirkstandard's
    Alternative, 2010)
*Harold* (Quirkstandard's Alternative, 2012)

For Children
*I Eat Squirrels* (Quirkstandard's Alternative, 2009)
*Fizzlebert Stump, The Boy Who Ran Away From The Circus
    (And Joined The Library)* (Bloomsbury, 2012)
*Fizzlebert Stump And The Bearded Boy* (Bloomsbury, 2013)

More information can be found at www.afharrold.com.

Acknowledgements

A few of these pieces appeared, sometimes in slightly different
forms, elsewhere: 'If There Is A Beginning' was previously published
in *Word Gumbo*; 'To Food' in *Ferment*; 'Pillow' in *Obsessed With Pipework*;
'The Good Book' in *The Nail*; 'On Burdens' in *14*; 'Summer Neglect' in
*Reading Poetry: An Anthology*; and 'Takeaway' in *Lung Jazz: Young British
Poets For Oxfam*.

# Contents

Part II.

# The First Lesson

*Its eggs are hidden through the world,*
*like nits, like gnats' eggs – invisible things,*
*tiny things, tucked in books, in leaves –*
*they hatch, they hatch, they hatch.*

# Part I.

*Death, like the sun, cannot be viewed directly;*
*it is like an unfathomable void that gives us a sort*
*of metaphysical vertigo if we so much as go near*
*the edge of the cliff.*
— 'On Embalming', from *Notes Of An Anatomist*, F. Gonzalez-Crussi

# If There Is A Beginning

It began with a message on the phone in early May.
It began long before that too, of course, many times.

It began when my father died.
It began when the cats died off, one by one.

It began with the death of Ben Kenobi –
though that turned out to be a cheat, a glowing ghostlife.

It began in books – it began with Noël Coward
on the floor of the bathroom at Firefly, in three biographies.

It began with Gertrude Lawrence in those same biographies,
suddenly dead –

I think of them meeting (he thirteen, she fifteen),
she taking him upstairs, he being unimpressed by it all

but loving her for forty years, nonetheless –
the news broken at the races by a back page's Stop Press.

It began with Frodo and Bilbo taking the ship into the West,
but more it began with Sam, left to watch them go,

left to turn around and go back home and just get on
with life.

It began with so many things –
with Peake's final shaky years – with silence coming down.

And once aware of closing books,
of the shadow the hero never sees flit by

there's been no escape, no real escape for long. So,
it began with a phone message at the start of May –

*She's going in for tests tomorrow* – and not the sort,
I thought, you can revise for in advance.

## To The Consultant

How many years of trekking,
of book-study and walking wards,
of prodding ungiving flesh and smiling,
of shaking quietly the hand that shakes ...

how long ago did you set out
hand-wringing down antiseptic corridors,
through doors that swung as easily shut
as open, through doors that only let
those called by name inside ...

how far is it you've come,
down years and years,
since your mother pushed you out
headlong on this dreadful trajectory to end with us?

# Geriatric Ward

*i.*

It's that wallpaper –
that and the sense we're all going down,
that the nurses chuckle tiredly in cubbyholes
shifting deckchairs.

That bloody wallpaper
(its ugly half-metallic floral sheen covering one wall
as if to cover more would be undue extravagance)
is battered – beside your head strips dangle,

not knocked horizontally
as the porters wheeled your bed around,
but vertically, like the silk inside a coffin lid
of some poor bugger sent too early underground.

*ii.*

Your back's to the wallpaper.
You face down the ward
at five old biddies who mutter and grumble.

They poke out from blankets like turtle heads –
myopic, tectonic and frail as sand.
You smell it every time one takes a shit.

To your right's a window –
two red brick walls that make a view,
black netting one floor up keeps pigeons out.

Below a generator rumbles on,
day and night, keeping lights and lives alight.
And if you stretch there's one small scrap of blue
that prisoners, and you, might call the sky.

# The Worst Thing

The worst thing I did, I did to you.

When you began the conversation saying
*It isn't good news, they've found ...*
at that precise moment I wrote you off.

An in-case-of-fire blast door dropped shut,
I switched to neutral,
said inside that you were gone, done, dusted.

And at that instant was born a traitor to you.

# Blackbird

This morning my favourite bird
(so simply named)
stopped me in the car park.

An ink-blot on the white stripe.
Identifiable by a papery triangle flap –
yellow bill in tar-black feather, shocked red guts.

The crunch of car-on-bird hit my mind's ear.

At that moment, right then, you lay alive in bed –
oxygenated, awaiting a new round of visitors.

Half ashamed I recognised a fact: this bird –
hours dead – had already made me think of you.

# Name An Old Shame

When I was five or six
I denied you to your face.
I claimed I wasn't yours.
I was adamant on the point.

I said I'd been adopted,
cuckooed into your nest,
come from another planet
off out in outer space.

It wasn't a joke to me,
this truth had trumped it all.
I was waiting for the night
I'd head off home at last.

Today I still remember
that foreign planet's name,
embarrassingly bizarre,
but true, I called the place:

*Donkey.*
          I know, I know,
I hide my face in shame.
You'd think a poet's head
would bubble better names.

So, now I'm sorry Mum,
for this early odd betrayal.
An awful thing to do:
which, besides, turned out untrue.

# CT

Information is our ally.
To know a thing's name helps.
I've always liked hearing explanations.

They send you for another scan: they like information too.
The technician who injects the dye says,
*You'll feel as if you're going to wet yourself, but you won't.*

You confirm this,
add how you find yourself growing hot,
down to your toes – like hemlock in reverse.

But I find I can only think of the midwife
who swings the brand new baby up, not saying,
*You'll feel as if you're going to live forever, but you won't.*

# Dog

A cat finds a corner,
accurately ashamed of its need to excrete,
but your dog shits square in public,
anywhere, without looking back.

Hot beige-brown cylinders sliced by peristaltic spasms,
an inverted map of her stinking bowels,
that I stoop to pick up.

And this is the dog that turned away from you
six months before the doctors did their tests –
refused to share the room with you,
begrudged your strokes, showed you the shoulder,
but never once said what it was that upset her so.

Of course, I'd be an idiot to blame her for that,
dumb thing as she is, but I'm afraid I am and do.

# Growing Dark

You slink off to bed at eight o'clock
(half-unlike the mink or mouse)
and leave me in the hunting dusk
to feel the silence fill the house.

All day long you've longed to go,
to creep away and shut your eyes.
I sit with curtains open and
stand look-out as the daylight dies.

# To Food

You taught me well, to scan a menu
and choose, not the biggest price tag,
but the biggest plate – a trait I keep up,
or try to. Unlike you.

I drape an imaginary towel over one arm
to bring your orders to your chair –
a little fruit, pre-chopped, a little juice.

The kitchen's my domain,
the fridge organised in date order.

As days become weeks I note how halves
become quarters, become morsels,
become even less – until, almost, a breath of air,

a cup of light, the smell of subliming ice.

# Opening

He's in the house, it seems.
In other rooms for now,
but making plans to enter this one where you wait.

He's swept the kitchen,
leeched life from the fridge, the oven –
left the crockery lying unused.

He's roamed the garden –
left things gasping for water,
let weeds tangle themselves beyond my means to cut back.

And day by day, sitting there in that one chair,
practising the revelation of the skeleton,
I watch you opening your arms to him.

# Bumblebee, Late Summer

I'm on hands and knees.
She crawls blade by blade,
up and down, all at sea, across the lawn –
this red-tailed bumblebee, fat and slow.

However close I loom, lean in to see,
I'm still nothing to her.

You're going for three, four lie-downs in one day,
in one afternoon some days –
it seems desperate to me.

This bumblebee could take to the wing,
but instead insists on hoofing it,
a pilgrim on her knees, toward hibernation:

her burrow, her bed, her whole new year ahead.

# Summer Neglect

Things go on growing in your garden,
but order decays. Borders grow old
and ragged, grow green. Thorny arms
reach out for ledges, for hands to hold.

Colour fades as leafy things spring up.
The human patterns grow rare. Thinking
gives way to nature. The pond evaporates,
a damp ring-mark on stones, daily sinking.

# All Streets In Time

We took you up to hospital
in the back of an ambulance one time.
A bad day, a worse night and so this.

You got a compliment, at least.
The paramedic, fumbling his needle,
unable to find an entry point

described your veins as
(I quote) *small and delicate.*
You never were a small and delicate woman.

It was a rattling ride back there.
I spent my time hanging on,
reading labels:

*razor, swabs, burns kit, maternity kit, sterile water.*
There was a chart: *Cardiac Chest Pain Pathway.*
At the bottom it read SUITABLE FOR PHT –

in a glance I read it as PITY.
I thought of Larkin's
'all streets in time are visited'.

He got the needle into you eventually.
A syringe driver clanked, whirred,
drove salt water in.

You looked at me over your blanket,
oxygen tubes and a half-weak smile.
Sorry to be a nuisance.

Outside streets whizzed by,
traffic parted,
and we were unloaded,

rolled into A & E,
where you were laid out ready for the long wait.
And in my rush I forgot to pick up anything to read.

# Via Dolorosa

*i.*

If I could take on me your pain,
take that weight that's made you look so old,
and carry it myself a way, like Simon did,
or even simply share –
link our bodies up
and be a part of this slow sloping journey:
share sicknesses and boredom,
hear your clots short-breath my lungs –
if this chance were offered me, you know,
without a moment's hesitation,
I wouldn't take it.

Like Winston Smith I'm afraid, I'm ashamed.

It's here, at the point of inconvenience, my cowardice begins.

*ii.*
Another day and it's bollocks to all that.

Of course I'd take it on,
of course swap beds, take up your plastic mattress.
I'd take hospitals and lymphomas,
indignity, doctors and the showing skull.
Christ, for you I'd take it all and not think twice.

And thinking this I wonder if, at last,
after so many false starts and misunderstandings,
I've put my finger on what love is.

What else could this feeling token?
I sit quiet.
And then I see the imagined me laid out in bed,

and you at my bedside.

# Come Hear The Band

That afternoon we sat and talked
frankly, grimly, without shame,
facing up to what's to come:
the future's dark, the future's flame.

When we'd had this chat with dad,
years ago, when he went too,
he'd hardly paused for thought before:
'Louis Armstrong's *Black And Blue*.'

When, at last, the big day came
you'd vetoed it, sent it back,
picked another song instead:
'You've seen your dad, he wasn't black.'

Louis' voice rasped out instead
a Waller song and *Cabaret*:
For what is life in front of death?
It said a thing we'd want to say.

I asked you for your music choice,
what would be your last request?
I'd keep that *Cabaret* to close,
but you could guide me on the rest.

You didn't know, couldn't think,
in time I left you lying there.
Caught the bus to take me home.
My pocket buzzed and out the air

a message flew between our phones,
I read it, laughed, was proud of how
ten minutes with the radio
had thrown up Queen's *Don't Stop Me Now*.

# Two Texts

*i.*

Overwhelmed by visitors who overstay your strength
you put on your glasses, thumb open your phone –

*The world and his wife*, you mean to type, but,
perhaps predictably, a different message flies –

*The world and his wolf have visited*, you say.
It's by such mistakes the truth is known.

*ii.*

I'm not angry at death, it will come to us all,
just at its incompetence, all this hanging around.

I open the dictionary when I get home,
to answer the question you'd earlier asked –

*Why must the patient be so patient?*
You'd rung your bell: an unanswered sound.

The word's from French, go far enough Greek:
from *pathos, to suffer*. So truth is unmasked,

understanding is reached. I send you a text.
By return you fly back: *You can say that again.*

# To Avoid Cross-Infection

My hands have never been this clean:
at every junction, by every door,
those plastic pots enticing me
to lather them with alcohol.

It's a habit I've grown accustomed to:
I stop, I pause, I squirt some out.
I rub my palms, wring my hands:
the comic villain surveys his loot.

I anoint myself beyond the wrist.
I take a second squirt for luck,
and then, here comes the bit I like:
it's damp, it's cold, it's lifting up.

It's transubstantiated soap,
changed to breath upon my skin.
Oh, now I'm free to touch the sick,
my hands have never been so clean.

# Staring Sketch

I stare at you so long that I get lost,
or you get lost.

Whatever scale stood between us lifts,
and I'm referenceless –

you're a world, enormous but so far away,
and I'm taking all day

to take you in,
the still eyelids, the touching lips, the still skin.

I'm taking so long to reach you,
like Apollo flying three days to the bright blank moon,

I've stared so long, the destination's changed,
inside this brainpan you're unmoved but rearranged.

A simple way of sending the familiar alien –
like saying a word again and again.

Your face is made fresh,
the still eyelids, the touching lips, the soft flesh:

a perfect picture I could never make.
If I were a wishing man, I'd wish you'd never wake.

# Pillow

Every electric light has a switch.
Usually it's on the wall nearby,
sometimes you'll find another room
with control panels and labelled buttons.
But there's always a switch somewhere.

Every candle is put out by a draught of air,
whether from mouth, window or door;
or by a conical snuffer lowered carefully;
or a pinch of licked finger and thumb;
or by letting it burn down, run out of wick and wax.

You sleep in the middle of the day.
The sun might as well be the moon.
I anticipate you waking again,
the muggy swell of nausea, of living beyond your means,
and I look at the pillow, that simple snuffer.

How easy would it be? How hard?
Would you come to before it was done,
push back, thrash weakly and weaker?
Or would it, like morphine, be absorbed in a dream,
closing curtains, a shush of librarian walking away?

# Dignity

*i.*

Months before any of this happened
I was visiting
and we, sat up at night, were talking.

I'd watched a programme
about the long slow foggy slide into dementia
and said to you – *Don't do that –*
*don't linger on and on like that –*
*when you go, make it quick – a car crash, say –*
*something sudden – over, done.*

And you, who worked with the sliding,
agreed, but said – *It'll be pills, if anything.*

We left the conversation there, over, done,
understanding the importance of good timing.

*ii.*

And now, months after all this began,
I visit you,
and sit and talk and look and listen.

The doctor's at your bedside,
rearranging medication again, more deckchairs.
And you tell her – *I want it over now.*
*If there were just a button I could press …*

This hospital is full of such buttons,
but they're all locked away and out of reach.

I watch in boredom now.
The joke has lingered on too long
without the punch-line turning up.

The secret of dying well? No secret, I think – timing.

## Abandon Hope All Ye

Getting off at Redhill station
I catch a bus to your hospital,
asking the driver for a return.

He looks up blankly and says,
as if it were an obvious thing,
they don't do return tickets.

# Post-Mortem Continuo

It would be nice to be of use afterwards:
lend a kidney out, a vein, cornea, heart –
spread oneself thinly among the needy;

or have one's hip or shoulder mounted up,
a pistoned car driven into it at speed –
let's slo-mo the impact, make the roads safer;

or even spend the years lying out at Knoxville,
just rotting down at one's own pace, outside –
helping forensics with their enquiries.

Science has a better breed of afterlife
than that dished out by your religious pals.
To be of use, to save a life or two –
less selfish than the *me, me, me* of eternity.

## Pond, Late Autumn

Fish seek out the sunlight.
In that one corner
they're clustered like marbles on a tilted floor.

Nine tenths of the pond is shadow
and they don't go there,
except for darting misadventures.

They're soon home again,
back to the speechless company
who didn't miss them and who tread water
with feathered fins, dully, daintily,
basking like the sharks they dream themselves to be –
wishing pondweed to reefs
and an English autumn to anywhere else.

# Defeated

You wouldn't die, for so long.
But you wouldn't live, lost interest,
bored of it all.

The hospice had everything,
all channels of entertainment
were open and available:

DVDs, TV, radio piped to your bed;
ask for a magazine, for a book,
they'd bring it to you.

But no.
The rot had caught your idea of yourself,
laid you in a corner like a rank winter bear.

You trusted the feel of yourself,
trusted the doctor's prediction.
Took off your glasses and waited for darkness.

Take a photo every hour
and the world rushes by:
nurses are blurs,

flowers open, bloom, wilt,
the bed beside you fills and empties,
people moan and weep, curtains snap shut.

You're the silent central stone,
the pivot around which it all revolves:
a dull still small lump under an extra blanket.

You stayed so long,
not dying,
you were Mother of the Hospice.

I'd visit each day,
you'd humour me by answering the crossword clues.
I had as little as you to say.

# Hospice Song

You know there came a time I hated you?
When all my patient waiting seemed in vain?
When I made that daily train ride for the view
of you laid out in boredom and dull pain,
tipped up with nausea among the dying?

Each day they wheeled them out. You remained,
against your will and turned to face the wall,
seceding from your stringy corpse so drained
which at that darkling edge had come to stall,
your soundtrack just the driver's sighing.

I'd been there with you when your name was called.
I'd shared that final doctor's words with you:
no two ways out, her news was somewhat bald,
you and the bloody world would soon be through.
August then, you'd match the summer's sinking.

But autumn turned to winter, to be crude,
in a sick parade of nothing much at all:
repeated bowls of half-dismembered food
and yellow bile to top it up to full.
You lying there, a six foot woman shrinking.

Like Captain Oates it seemed as if you'd crawled
away across the wilderness of bed,
and left me there to sit it out, appalled,
beside the hunch of bone and feathered head.
Half hour duty done and I'd be leaving.

To find you still alive, well, that I dreaded,
almost more than finding you had gone.
You knew, and I, just where all this was headed.
We cursed this body that hung around so long:
a shoddy box from which your life was leaking.

I felt betrayed, felt bitter, I felt wronged:
as if you'd failed to keep a simple promise.
My mother, mum, you held the magic wand,
you made things right, you shouldn't have a weakness.
The secret shared: you were a human being.

Too tired to fight you raised no raging fist:
just lay abed, a monumental bore,
a waste of time and space ... you get the gist.
Your garden under snow held out for thaw,
but cancer had you beat and you were fleeing.

I'd sit beside you sometimes as you snored,
I'd wonder how it all had come to this:
so thin (at last! Weight Watchers would applaud),
the diet worked in that necropolis:
but not the slender sylph you'd been foreseeing.

Each day, upon goodbye, I Judas-kissed:
I dared that mark to be our last adieu.
My kiss designed, in love, to not be missed
by Shadow-Death on its next wander through.
Death's snuffer is, at best, a kind of freeing.

# Electric Bed, December

You slept so much on your final fast,
drifting shut-eyed through days,
that I asked you once whether you dreamt.

Legs reduced to spindles,
bound to this bed
I was afraid for you.

The first dream you told me
had you as boss of some road-digging crew,
a gang of shirtless workmen
hammering away with drills
and shovels and barrows,
but
they weren't digging it straight.

The second dream you told me
had you in a hot air balloon
and
it was drifting off course.

The third dream you told me
had you home,
I guess,
because the fish had left the pond
and were flapping up the path,
as if dropped by a bird
or a sunk flood.

*Strange dreams*, you said.

The other thing I remember
was how you once described the hospice:
*A place where they wake you up at nine at night
in order to give you your sleeping pills.*

# The Reversal

The seesaw tilt of time
tipped me up,
tipped you down.

*Responsible adult* –
I stood behind the swings
ready to push you,

and I stood before the swings,
arms open,
ready to catch you,

and I stood at the edge of the rec,
the quiet boy,
waiting for his mother to fetch him.

# Not At Home

I've borrowed your home for months.
You went out one morning,
aren't back yet. It's a New Year.

My mess is limited to one room.
I wash up promptly, don't impose.
Occasionally I watch television.

Your newspaper's on the stool
beside your armchair, folded back,
open on the listings. September.

I hardly dare touch anything.
The postman brings your post.
New snow's wiped clean your lawn.

# Neighbours

My guess was we'd end up like Ken and Lou –
next door flats and shared teatimes.
A love-love hate-hate relationship unrolling years.

You weren't her, of course, and I'm not really him,
but all the same, something of the sort
unfolds in me as time gives way to fear –

a growing loneliness perhaps,
a hint of one true love against the growing dreary dark.
A knock – *Ashley? Are you home? Do you want your tea?*

It's a shock, for sure, to know for good
this half unhappy future's gone.
It's all on me, at last –
my long prevarication lived out
with bloody strangers lodged next door.

# On Perseverance

One day I couldn't come to see you.
The railway had stopped running.

The line was blocked by some old chap
who, in desperation, had driven
his motorised mobility scooter
off the platform and under a train.

I say *desperation*, but that's just a guess.

He survived
and a month later blocked the line again.

# The Good Book

*The Wind In The Willows* was a set text in our family,
read as some sort of salve or cure-all in hopeless cases.

Years back I caught you reading it in that hot white room,
sat in that long bed with the stickman man beside you.
Words marched on, as if to stop were to invite the final stop.

Could that brittle body have passed a comprehension test?
Were you wasting breath on gone deaf ears?

Perhaps it's not important. You sat and read
and he kept breathing for a time, that's all.
But now I've begun to worry myself –
I don't remember where it stops, how it ends:

when the coiling riot of weasel's ejected from the Hall,
or is there something after that? Spring cleaning,
summer on the river, another winter lost in the Wild Wood?

# April Sketch

Your cottage stands empty.
I pop by after the nursing home.

There is frog spawn.
Three large clumps dumped among the pondweed.

It says spring is here at last,
after the winter you didn't expect to survive.

A fortnight later I pass by again.
The spawn seems to have gone, but marsh marigolds

dash a brilliant border round the far bank.
The fish seem well-fed, despite our inattention.

The world's bragging how much more alive it is than
    you
balanced on your electric bed, starving away.

Everywhere trees meringue themselves for marriage.
Idly I wonder what the next sign will be.

Then, walking by the lake near my home,
it's sunset's nightingales, two of them, duelling.

# Have You Heard The One About …

When dad died his brain went first,
plugged through with tumours like sunlit spaces.
His body ticked on outside.

You've chosen the opposite route.
I think of Tithonus,
the Trojan consort of Eos, old Rose-Tinted Dawn.

She asked Zeus to help them out.
As a joke he gave the mortal chap eternal life,
but not eternal youth.

His body gave in and emptied out to age,
but mental continuity was maintained.
Shrunk to a raisin he became a talking cicada.

Sit on my shoulder, mum, I'm almost a real boy now.

# Doing The Sum

Regretting nothing
I count each loss on a finger,
move on to a new hand
and carry on counting.

Only by an act like this,
done in the morning as birds
peck seed from their feeder
and the postman whistles

somewhere nearby
on his slow way to me,
can I take true stock of what it is
that's added up across years

to reduce me to this man
wrapped up in this skin,
wound tight by memory –
to make that man exactly me.

# On Burdens

Among the many things I can't remember,
that first day at school,
those early Christmases,
my first successful cycle ride,
I can't recall your ever carrying me,
though, of course, you did.

I've no recollection of being up in your arms,
hefted like a wiggling weight,
a squirming sack squeezed against your breasts.

(I can remember seeing,
from the strapped seat of my push-chair,
that curved window of bottle-bottomed glass –
the betting shop dad left me out front of.)

At the end I could've lifted you up.

# Three Legs In The Evening

I'd heard of how tourists go to Giza,
seek out the Sphinx in her sandy bed
and are underwhelmed, unimpressed by her small, chipped head.

It's the same, I see, visiting the nearly dead:
remembering simply unprepares you, steals your breath.
Pillows shine like dunes, ask, *Is this her?*

# c. 7.30 pm May 6th 2010

On your last evening,
a slump dragged down the edge of your lip.

Gravity and cancer conspired against you.
One muscle lost its grip.

As I sat down you didn't turn.
You didn't turn to face me at all.

I slipped a finger into your hooked hand,
felt my warmth fight your palm's cool.

I asked if you were in pain.
You answered by rustling leaves,

your throat sounding a ghost language,
empty vowels snagged-sighing in trees.

I asked if you ached,
if you were just tired, and you nodded,

that skull that had regrown
its bird's covering of white down nodded.

And when I told you of my cowardice,
how I feared the world to come,

you brushed the tiniest of brushstrokes
across my finger with your thumb.

And soon after that I left you to the night,
to the long dark and to the fear,

and as I kissed you
your staring eye loosed a tear –

just one, clear as air,
as salt, I'll say, as the sea.

I can't know if it fell for yourself
or for me.

# The Core

When it comes again
it's just words
on a telephone line,

expected, awaited,

desired even.

But suddenly I'm cored,
like an apple shot through
and left an amazed torus.

I'm hollowed out,
no. Filled with sand,
no. Filled with stone,
no. Filled with wind,
no. Filled with light,
no. Filled with depth,
yes,

filled with depth,
but not profundity,
just a constant falling

like Alice down the rabbit hole
in the zero gee of a shuttle flight.

# The Last Room

How long was that last night? I can't think.
The sideways droop of lip had gone by morning.

We gave the nurses two boxes of chocolates
when we came to clear the room.

Was that the right thing to do?
You would have told us the right or wrong of it.

We filled a bin bag with what had accumulated –
half-full toiletries, knickers, get well cards,

that photo they'd taken against your will,
the hobby-bright box they'd had you paint.

They'd treated you like a child in their care.
For that I wanted to take back the chocolates.

# How It Happens

The technician waits an hour before looking in.
He has a spy-hole.

For a body the size you ended up
it could all be over in an hour and a half.

First the coffin lights up, then the flesh burns,
then the organs.

I don't know if the chemicals they used
while they stored you

add colours to the bonfire,
lend you some eerie flame-light grave-light.

I read the technician's account in a newspaper,
he didn't mention it.

When the flames are dead too
he rakes out the remains and they're left to cool

before he puts them into the cremulator,
where they're ground up between ball-bearings.

I'm not sure if that's a trademarked name or not,
but bits of bone are anathema at scatterings.

# Free Now

free now from friends, free to disappoint them
free now from promises, blameless to break them

free from career, free now from careering
you're freed from your family, freed up from caring

free from the seasons, from slow drifting changes
from day-follows-night-time, you're into eclipses

free now from food, I pocket your apple
free from your name, I pocket your name

free now from maps, you know no directions
free now from houses, you cannot come home

free now from holding, your hands hold nothing
free now from breathing, your lungs hold nothing
free now from looking, your eyes hold nothing
free now from longing, you've gone into fire

freed up from dust, you've gone now to dust
freed up from death, you've gone now to death

# For If You're Still Looking Down

Picking peanuts from a wooden bowl
after your father's funeral
I remember being accused, in a voice
that jabbed like she jabbed her stick,
of gluttony by my grandmother.

A small gluttony, for sure, but still
enough for her to find it unseemly,
unsightly perhaps, as if I were happy,
guzzling greedily, at the sombre affair.

*He's still watching you*, she said, pointing up.
I believed her neither then, nor now.

They'd always scared me, the pair of them,
in that constant cold little house,
wedged mid-terrace in treeless London,
that smelt of veg and Sunday stout.

And though, now, I know she was upset,
a lifetime's husband upped and gone,
not neatly either, ragged and cancerous,
I still half-resent that accusation.
After your cremation we encourage eating.

# The Fallen Oak

That fallen oak had continued to grow –
half its roots skywards as if to plumb clouds,
still leafing along the forest floor.

We stepped round it as your dog ran ahead,
picked our way up the slope until
you stopped us at the top and said
that this was where you'd let go his dust –
let his ash into the forest,
somewhere out of sight you might pass by
out walking the dog from time to time.

I'd never thought what had become of him –
that was your business.

Your business has become mine.

# A Constant Background Sense Of Sickness

It's like walking the plank, this nausea.
It's as if you've left me all at sea.
You've made a green sailor out of me –

pressed me, with your death, into a new role,
into a job I never interviewed for,
a position I feel under-qualified to fill.

My charts have grown suddenly empty –
I'm off in that unlikeable white space
where the mapmaker suffered cartographer's block.

It's not me that's unbalanced, it's the world.
Your weight lifted up a chimney
has set it wobbling, seeking equilibrium –

until it settles I'll live in fear of *here be dragons*.

# Takeaway

Waiting for my order in the takeaway
I can't help but overhear the little West Indian guy
(flat cap, squashed face, big tight voice)
bitching at the old white guy who said,
'I lost *my* wife to cancer a year ago … '
at the start of the conversation and nothing more.

It's a catalogue of misdiagnoses and misdirection,
of a lack of shared information,
of radio- and chemo- and bad results.
('She … ' this and 'She … ' that. *His* wife I guess.)
The nerves get burnt out, but no one had said.
He's close to breaking up.
I hear the wobble through the rich patois roll.

I huddle behind the TLS,
pretend to read a poem I can't keep a grip on.
He's got me almost in tears myself,
and I want to kneel down with him and say, 'I know'.
But I don't know.
An orphan's different to a husband on the precipice.

'She wanted to have her feet washed,'
he went on, letting the darkness out through cracks,
'but there was no one … '

# Wardrobe

You had so many clothes
it took a dozen black bags to bag them all up.

I wonder if they split them, sorted them,
sent them away out of consideration?

It would be my luck they'd end up in a shop here,
snapped up by some woman your size.

One day without thinking I'll touch her shoulder,
maybe hug her.

She'll stand startled,
but let the moment go just long enough

before coughing gently
and moving me on.

# Mother

Your touch on my life was light,
worse than absent, it was a net.
Like the conjuror catching the bullet
in her teeth, every wound was salved,
nudged aside or poulticed up with a kiss.

I didn't recognise this until later came.
Until the doctor's door shut on you,
and we sat down. You loved me so.
They must have special lectures on this,
on how to aim words so carefully.

# On Parents

At last they appear together in a dream,
and I wake from it with a true sense
that they've given me advice for going on,
tips and pointers on how to live a life
in this upland future they've gifted me.

And I sit up in bed, dazed, and realise
that I wasn't listening, I'd missed it all,
and outside noisy kids head off to school
and though the sun shines I haven't a clue
what I should do tomorrow or today.

# The Promise

When I am old I shall maintain my dignity, with luck,
avoid the hands of nurses, the sponges of carers
and set my own table for my own tea.

Whatever supermarket remains in that distant era
will deliver essential supplies twice a week:
whatever food is still available, whatever drugs I need.

With luck it will be the future we were promised as kids,
back when it shone brightly with chrome and flying suits,
shone from beyond adulthood's spreading horizon,

the future in which glimpsed cures have arrived
where we'll have the choice to live on or fade out
denied to our parents and theirs.

# Missing

I missed your birthday again.
Looked at the diary a day or two late,
realised it had slipped by.

Behind us
sharks move in darkness, at depth,
coming closer to shore.

Their jaws snap up,
remembering folds itself around a leg,
drags us down through beating blood.

But it's no good.
Missing this birthday's not a crime.
The wrong was already done.

The date I don't forget's on the other side,
when the year brimmed with life
and spring sourly sapped away your quick.

# Leo

*i.*

When I was five you got me a cat.
He was a kitten, but I don't remember him like that.

To me he's just a remarkable old tom,
keeps himself to himself, is as ginger as dawn.

Two flashes of personality leap to mind:
one, how he'd do handstands for a lick of melon rind;

and, two, that day he brought home a prize,
not common headless bird or exsanguinated mouse,

but a slab of uncooked steak,
stolen through someone's backdoor from an unguarded plate.

We cut it up for him, never mentioned it outside the house.

*ii.*

I'm thirty-six, writing this, and still see that cat.
Saw him last night in fact,

in a garden that appears
to be one I've not seen for something like nine years,

behind a house I've not lived in for eighteen,
with you, who's been gone for one.

He's visited before, has never grown dead,
just old.

He's become huge, dense and fragile,
like a moth-attacked awkward stuffed animal.

I'm afraid to pick him up in case he's stiff, like a dog.

*iii.*
Last night we sat there, you and I, and looked at him.
Did the maths in the afternoon sun:

thirty-six minus five.
A record-breaking cat to be so old and still alive.

Surprised by the facts, I didn't notice how wrong we'd
    been,
not until I'd woken and looked again,

and then it struck, and struck hard:
it's not the cat who walks my dreams who's got old,

it's me.

# Ann 824

Among the scattered poem-buds,
the scribbles and reviewer's notes,
my pocketbook is still home to
a handful of your lesser quotes.

(I'd make transcriptions on the bus,
or on the train of things you'd said,
verbatim notes, an inky scar
to keep me straight when you were dead –

else memory's a kindly thing
and fluid flows from shape to shape
and left unchallenged over time
its jaggy edges ease away.)

We'd wheeled you in through A&E
down to your room on Godstone Ward.
You sick of waiting, sick of sickness.
Long ago we'd both grown bored.

I won't repeat them in a poem,
the things you told me, things you said.
Although this book's one long betrayal
I'll give you peace there in that bed.

You'd spent your nights beside the phone,
an open-eared Samaritan
(at least before this cancer came
and clocked your number down to none);

you'd spent your years in social work,
providing respite care for those
who'd otherwise capsize with caring.
You never struck a saintly pose.

Then axe-blows echoed in your roots.
The cancer's clutch that slowed you down,
that, day by day, ate up your innards,
locked you in your dressing gown,

turned the known world inside out,
wine went salty, sweet went sour,
fire cold and day to dusk:
the carer was the cared for now.

*I've always been so independent* –
(divorced, widowed, survived: it's true).
Having filled a brimming sick bowl:
I'm *supposed to look after* you.

Oh mum, you did, remember when,
a week or so before you died,
in what was our last conversation,
you improved my shepherd's pie?

But mother, dear, you *were* a burden,
*that* fear of yours came sadly true:
your legs packed in, your muscles went,
too weak for anger you withdrew.

You weren't too proud to be a patient,
weren't stroppy, uncooperative,
but being helpless ate your heart up,
this was no way, you said, to live.

Alive you buttressed failing others,
the listening-eared Samaritan –
this book extends our conversation,
but your part's silent, dead and gone.

# Part II.

*I wish you hadn't*
*caught that cold, but the dead we miss are easier*
   *to talk to: with those no longer*
*tensed by problems one cannot feel shy and, anyway,*
   *when playing cards or drinking*
*or pulling faces are out of the question, what else is there*
   *to do but talk to the voices*
*of conscience they have become?*

— 'The Cave Of Making', W.H. Auden

# Get Over It

She's passed away, gone out the room, drawn the curtains.
She's stepped outside, might be some time.

She's snuffed it, clocked off, left the building.
She's pegged out, is feeding worms, gone up the chimney.

She's put on the big overcoat. She's filed her last report,
has finished her homework, put down her paintbrush.

She's kicking up the daisies from six feet under,
has sent the bucket flying, has dropped the baton.

She's left the farmer one hand short for harvest,
made paperwork for the doctor, given the undertaker overtime.

She's paid the piper, paid the ferryman, paid the price.
She's stopped making plans, stopped making sense,
    has switched off the lights.

She's shut the last book, has finished the cryptic crossword.
Her record's stopped spinning, her radio's reporting static.

She's struck out for *wherever*, she's joined the statistics,
she's helping the angels with their enquiries.

She's slipped into the Country of Unconcern, she's not coming
    back.
She has moved away, has no more regrets, has spoilt my weekend.

She's been removed from the DNA Database,
has been deleted, is showing a 404 error.

She's been uploaded, downgraded, downsized.
She's been discontinued, dismissed, has disappeared.

She's met her maker, met the inevitable, met with misfortune.
She's turned up her toes, turned her nose to the wall, is
     keeping quiet.

She's gone swimming, grown forgetful, has slipped into night.
She has ceased to be a productive member of society.

She's caught a cold, collapsed the wave function,
has gone with the flow, gone with the undertow, gone off.

She's got beautiful plumage, she's fallen off her perch.
She's passed her sell-by date, the blue tits have had her cream.

She's walking with dinosaurs, teaching dodos to fly,
has found the lost chord, is dancing to a different drum.

She's fallen asleep, has answered the call, has gone for her tea.
She's been marked *return to sender*. She's heard the call of the
     wild.

Her train's jumped its tracks, has run out of coal,
     run out of steam,
has been cancelled, no longer serves this route, has departed
     early.

She's giving us the cold shoulder, is avoiding responsibilities,
is behind the bike-sheds, under the yew tree,
     through the lychgate.

She's running late, has passed Go, has collected two hundred
     pounds.
She's come unstuck, she's all dressed up with nowhere to go.

She's gone West, gone to a better place, gone for a burton.
She's gone exploring, gone fishing, gone to the rainbow's end.

She's gone aloft, gone away, gone forward,
has gone home, gone to grass, is out of sight, is having a kip,

has cut the cable, unknotted the painter, is set adrift.
She's given up the ghost, has closed her eyes, checked out
    the hotel.

She's sat in Banquo's chair, she's eaten Borgia's dinner.
She's sipped the wine of eternity, drunk the waters of Lethe.

She's painting the town black, has put her worst foot
    forward.
She's ticked the boxes, skipped tomorrow, cleared her diary.

She's solved the big equation, she's bitten the dust,
she's drawn a blank, she's breathed her last.

She's bought the farm, has faded away, has dropped off the
    twig.
She's left the back door open and let the cold weather in.

She's answered the summons, has heard the last trump.
She's gone before, she's moved on, has left town.

She's passed through passport control. She's airborne now.
She's off on a cruise, she's having a terribly big adventure.

She's walked by herself into a dark kingdom.
She's gone off the map, taken a real wrong turn.

She's underground. She's wearing her Sunday best.
She's at peace, she's having the big sleep, she's been made
    new.

She's been kissed by the maiden, has kissed the scythe,
has heard the whistle out in the long grass.

She's joined the great majority, has paid nature's debt,
has had her last waltz, had her last meal, taken her last bow.

She's passed beyond the veil, to the other side of the Styx,
to the other side of the Great Divide, she's passed over.

She's scored the home run, hit a six, converted the big try.
She's seen the chequered flag, has breasted the tape, won the race.

She's started having her post forwarded upstairs.
She's gone straight to voicemail, is the other side of the firewall.

Her clock has stopped, her watch has stopped,
her spring's wound down, her caesium atom no longer vibrates.

She's returned to ashes. She's returned to dust.
She's not answering the phone. She's forgotten her address.

She has ceased to be. She's withdrawn from the race.
She's walked the plank, gone the way of all flesh.

Farmer Todd has ploughed her under,
Sweeney Todd has sent her downstairs,

Brother Todd has taken her under his wing.
She's stopped working, she's retired, has run out of juice.

She's flown out of the high window of the old meadhall,
out into the unknowable night from whence she came.

Your mum is dead, get over it.

# Postscript

*I have looked at these poems,*
*looked back at them*
*and at the writing of them,*
*and can only think of what Wittgenstein*
*said about the* Tractatus,

*how he wrote to von Ficker*
*explaining that it consists of two parts:*
of the one which is here,
and of everything which I have not written.

And precisely this second part, *he went on,*
is the important one.

Two Rivers Press has been publishing in and about Reading since 1994. Founded by the artist Peter Hay (1951–2003), the press continues to delight readers, local and further afield, with its varied list of individually designed, thought-provoking books.